LIVE LIKE AN

Ancient Egyptian

DISCOVERING THE SECRETS OF THE ANCIENT EGYPTIANS

CLAIRE SAUNDERS

ILLUSTRATED BY
RUTH HICKSON

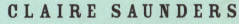

Button
BOOKS

CONTENTS

WHO WERE THE ANCIENT EGYPTIANS?

The ancient Egyptian civilization began about 5,000 years ago around the River Nile in the northeastern corner of Africa. It lasted for over 3,000 years, and was one of the world's first great civilizations, with magnificent monuments, writing and beautiful art.

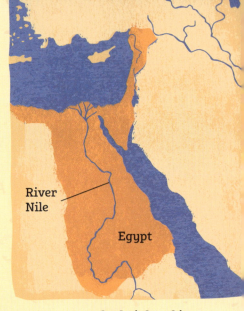

Egypt at the height of its power in about 1200 BCE.

River Nile

Egypt

The Black Land

Ancient Egypt owed its life to the great River Nile, the world's longest river, which flowed through Egypt's rocky, rainless desert. Each year it flooded its banks, leaving behind a layer of rich black silt that was perfect for growing crops. The people called their land Kemet – the Black Land – after this life-giving mud.

Pharaohs and gods

Egypt was ruled by kings or queens called pharaohs, who built grand tombs and monuments for themselves, and temples to honour the gods. Keeping the gods happy was important to the people of ancient Egypt – they worshipped over 2,000 gods and goddesses!

An ancient Egyptian friend

My name is Dedu. I am 10 years old and I live with my family in a great city in Kemet – the most beautiful place on earth! My father is a doctor, and one day I will be one too. First though, I have to finish school. I need to be able to read and write so I can learn all the skills and magic spells to cure people's illnesses. Let me show you around my home. You can visit my school, go boating on the river with my family and meet my pet cat, Miu! Come, and I will tell you about my life.

The Egyptian legacy

Here are a few of the amazing achievements of the ancient Egyptians:

Art and architecture
The Egyptians built incredible pyramids and other monuments, which have lasted for thousands of years. They were skilled artists too, and their tombs, temples and palaces were decorated with spectacular paintings and sculptures.

Pyramids at Giza

Writing system
Ancient Egyptian is one of the world's oldest written languages. The Egyptians used picture symbols, called hieroglyphs, to write words and sounds.

Calendar
Using their knowledge of the stars and moon, the Egyptians created a calendar that's very similar to the calendar we use today, with 365 days and 12 months. Each month had 30 days, with five extra days at the end of the year.

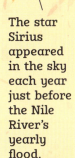

The star Sirius appeared in the sky each year just before the Nile River's yearly flood.

Finding evidence

How do we know how the people of ancient Egypt lived? A lot of evidence has come from their burial tombs, some of which were decorated with paintings of everyday life and filled with objects such as clothes, food and board games. The remains of a few abandoned villages have also survived, and Egyptian writing has been found carved and written on stone, papyrus and other surfaces.

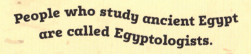

People who study ancient Egypt are called Egyptologists.

TIMELINE OF THE ANCIENT EGYPTIANS

The ancient Egyptians were around for over 3,000 years – a very long time! In fact, the last queen of Egypt, Cleopatra, lived closer to our own age than she did to the time of the early Egyptians, when the pyramids at Giza were built.

c.3100 BCE

Egypt is united for the first time when a king called Menes joins together two kingdoms, Upper Egypt and Lower Egypt. He makes Memphis the capital.

Egypt under the pharaohs

Egyptian history is divided into blocks of time called 'Periods' and 'Kingdoms'. Three of the most important are the Old Kingdom, the Middle Kingdom and the New Kingdom. During these time spans, Egypt flourished under powerful pharaohs. In between, there were unstable periods of weak rulers, in-fighting and foreign invasions, when the kingdom fell apart.

Lower Egypt

Memphis

Upper Egypt

c.1938 BCE

Mentuhotep II reunites Egypt after a period of civil war, and moves the capital to Thebes. He is the first ruler of the Middle Kingdom – a period of great architecture, art and crafts.

Predynastic Egypt (5300–3100 BCE)

Old Kingdom (c.2575–2130 BCE)

Middle Kingdom (c.1938–1630 BCE)

From 8,000 BCE

People begin to settle, build homes and farm in the Nile Valley.

c.2550 BCE

Pharaoh Khufu builds himself a huge royal tomb: the Great Pyramid at Giza. For the next 3,800 years, it will be the tallest human-made structure on Earth! Later, his son and grandson build their own pyramids nearby.

Hatshepsut

c.1332 BCE
Tutankhamun becomes pharaoh, aged nine. In 1922, his treasure-filled tomb is discovered in the Valley of the Kings.

c.1550 BCE
The start of the New Kingdom. This is Egypt's golden age, when it is at its biggest and most powerful.

c.1500 BCE
Pharaohs begin to be buried at the Valley of the Kings, in hidden-away tombs carved out of the rock.

332 BCE
Alexander the Great conquers Egypt, and founds the city of Alexandria. From now on, Egypt is ruled by Greek-Egyptian pharaohs.

Macedonian and Ptolemaic Egypt
(332 BCE–30 BCE)

New Kingdom
(c.1550 BCE–c.1075 BCE)

c.1075–332 BCE
Egypt is in decline. Invaders from the Nubian kingdom of Kush and from the Assyrian and Persian empires seize control at different times.

30 BCE
The last Greek-Egyptian pharaoh, Cleopatra, is defeated by the Romans. Egypt becomes part of the Roman Empire.

c.1473–1458 BCE
The peaceful and prosperous rule of Hatshepsut, a famous female pharaoh. Artworks show her dressed like a man and wearing a pharaoh's beard.

c.1279–1213 BCE
The rule of the great Ramesses II. He battles the Hittites and puts up statues of himself all over Egypt.

MAP OF ANCIENT EGYPT

Ancient Egypt grew up around the River Nile, which flowed from Upper Egypt in the south to Lower Egypt in the north. Most people lived in a narrow strip of land on either side of the river. Beyond this was the inhospitable desert.

At Abu Simbel in Upper Egypt four giant statues of Ramesses II, each 20 metres (66 feet) tall, guard the entrance to the main temple.

Trade and war

Ancient Egypt was a wealthy trading hub. Sometimes it traded peacefully with its neighbours, exchanging its plentiful grain for things it did not have, such as wood, oils, wines and incense. Other times it seized land by force, expanding the mighty Egyptian empire.

Key:
Cities ●
Places of interest ●

Goods from Egypt

- Gold
- Linen
- Glazed pottery
- Precious stones
- Furniture
- Grain

Goods to Egypt from Israel, Lebanon and Jordan

- Wood
- Wine
- Silver
- Copper
- Oil
- Slaves

Goods to Egypt from Nubia

- Gold
- Wildcat skins
- Ivory
- Spices
- Incense
- Exotic animals
- Slaves

Mediterranean Sea

Alexandria

Lower Egypt

Hittite, Assyrian and Persian empires

Memphis

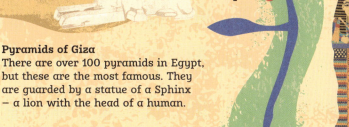

Pyramids of Giza
There are over 100 pyramids in Egypt, but these are the most famous. They are guarded by a statue of a Sphinx – a lion with the head of a human.

Valley of the Kings and Valley of the Queens
These two valleys are home to the tombs of New Kingdom pharaohs and their families. New tombs are still being discovered today.

Red Sea

Deir-el-Medina
The workmen who built and decorated the tombs in the Valley of the Kings lived in this village. It's now an important archaeological site that tells us how ordinary Egyptians lived.

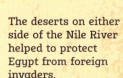

Karnak temple
This vast temple complex was added to by different pharaohs over thousands of years.

Thebes (modern-day Luxor)

River Nile

Upper Egypt

The unfinished obelisk
Egyptian obelisks were tall pillars carved from a single block of stone and decorated with hieroglyphics. This unfinished obelisk was found in an ancient granite quarry near Aswan.

The deserts on either side of the Nile River helped to protect Egypt from foreign invaders.

Aswan

Nubia

Abu Simbel

The land of Nubia began just south of Aswan. Sometimes the two neighbours were at peace, sometimes at war. Egypt ruled Nubia, on and off, for many centuries, controlling important trade routes. Later, the Nubian kingdom of Kush ruled Egypt for a time too.

EGYPTIAN SOCIETY

Ancient Egypt was divided into strict social groups based on people's jobs. The pharaoh and his court were at the top of society, and lowly peasants were at the bottom. There was very little movement between groups — if you were born a farmer, you would probably stay a farmer. Everyone believed that was the natural order of things.

Myth-busting: slaves

For a long time it was thought that the pyramids were built by slaves. But this is a myth! They were actually built by skilled labourers. Slavery in Egypt only really began from about the Middle Kingdom. Most slaves were foreigners captured in wars. Some worked as servants or labourers, others as skilled craftspeople.

In some ways, Egyptian peasants did not have much more freedom than slaves. Farmers were tied to land belonging to the pharaoh and big temples, and had to give up a share of their crops and do what they were told — a bit like serfs in medieval Europe.

Women in Egypt

Women had the same legal rights as men. They could do business, earn wages, own and inherit property, and marry who they wanted. But women and men were not completely equal. Women were expected to manage the home, while men held the important government jobs, including the top job — female pharaohs were very rare.

No one was more important than the pharaoh – to his people, he was a living god. His main jobs were keeping the gods happy and fighting wars to protect the kingdom and make it richer.

Pharaoh

The vizier was the pharaoh's second in command. Helped by an army of officials, he was in charge of the day-to-day running of Egypt.

Priests and priestesses were some of the wealthiest people in society. They looked after the temples and performed religious rituals.

Vizier, Officials, Priests and Priestesses

As few as 1% of people in ancient Egypt could read and write, so scribes were very important. They recorded all kinds of information and helped keep the kingdom running.

Becoming a soldier was a rare opportunity to move up in the world. Any man could join the army, and with skill, bravery and a bit of luck they could rise through the ranks and become quite wealthy.

Scribes, Soldiers

Craftspeople made all the things that people needed, from pots to wigs. Some craftspeople were quite well off, for example those who made luxury goods for high-ranking Egyptians.

Craftspeople, Merchants

Most of the people living in ancient Egypt were farmers or unskilled workers.

Fishermen, Servants, Labourers, Farmers

LIFE ON THE NILE

The River Nile was at the heart of ancient Egyptian life. Most people lived by its banks, fished in its waters and farmed the land on either side. There was usually always plenty of food to go around for everyone. Farming helped to make Egypt rich!

The Seasons

The Egyptians divided their year into three seasons:

Akhet (from July) Heavy rains caused the River Nile to flood its banks, covering the fields with water. People celebrated the arrival of the yearly flood with festivals.

Peret (from October) When the water fell, it left behind a thick layer of fertile mud. Farmers planted their seeds in this rich soil.

Shemu (from April) Harvest time! If the Nile had flooded just the right amount, there would be a good harvest. Every year, people made offerings to Hapi, the god of the Nile flood, hoping the level of the flood water would not be too low or high: too little flooding meant a poor harvest, while too much washed away people's homes.

The stems of the papyrus plant were used to make many things, from baskets, rope and sandals to a paper-like material for writing on.

Harvested grain was stored in grain stores. The government set aside enough grain to feed the people of Egypt in hard times.

The river was the main highway for people and goods — travel by water was much faster than routes through the desert. Large wooden boats transported goods from foreign lands, stone from quarries, animals, grain and other foods.

The river teemed with fish. Fishermen made simple boats or rafts from papyrus and fished using nets and sometimes spears.

Watch out! Crocodiles and hippos were a constant danger. A hippo could easily capsize a boat, and crocodiles sometimes snatched young children from the riverbank.

The main crops were emmer wheat and barley. To irrigate their fields, farmers dug channels to divert water from the river, or used tools like the shaduf. This invention lifted water in a bucket at the end of a pole.

River mud was mixed with sand and straw to make mud bricks, which were left to bake and harden in the sun. Most buildings were made from mud bricks.

INSIDE AN EGYPTIAN HOUSE

Most people lived in small, simple houses, where large families shared a few rooms. In the countryside, homes were usually single-storey and had small vegetable gardens, while in some towns, they were taller and built closer together. This picture shows a typical house where a fairly well-off family might have lived.

Most houses were built of mud bricks, which were cheap and plentiful. The small, high windows didn't let in much light, which helped to keep the house cool. Some houses were painted white to reflect the sun.

Lots of important activities, such as spinning and weaving, took place outside the home in the street.

Archaeologists have found 'false doors' set into the walls of some houses. This could have been because ancient Egyptians believed that dead ancestors would be able to visit through these doors.

Some homes had a shrine, where the family made offerings to gods that were important to the household.

People gathered in the living room to eat and sometimes sleep. Most Egyptian homes didn't have much furniture. Clothing and other belongings were stored in chests or boxes.

People sometimes slept on the flat roof, where it was cooler. Canopies made from woven reeds provided shade in the daytime.

Wealthy Egyptian homes

The houses of rich Egyptians had many more rooms, including big spaces for entertaining. Walls and ceilings were decorated with beautiful paintings, and a large garden held trees, flowers and a pool.

The kitchen yard was at the far end of the house. It had a clay oven for cooking food and a grindstone for grinding up grain into flour.

Cats were a favourite pet. People sometimes also kept geese or ducks for eggs, pigs and goats for meat and milk, and a dog to guard the house.

At nighttime, people rolled out mats or slept on ledges. Only wealthy people had beds. Instead of pillows, people used headrests made of wood, pottery or ivory.

Most people washed in the river or used a bowl of water. To go to the toilet, they dug a hole in the ground or used a pot filled with sand, which had to be emptied. Some pots had toilet seats on top, made of wood or limestone.

Some food and water was stored in pots and baskets below ground to keep it cool.

CHILDHOOD AND FAMILY LIFE

Family was very important in ancient Egypt. Parents cherished their children, and the birth of a new baby girl or boy was a happy occasion. Children were expected to have pride in their families and to respect their parents and look after them in old age.

Learning for life

Egyptian children had time for playing and having fun. But they also spent time learning all the things they would need to know as adults. Most children followed in their parents' footsteps and did the same job.

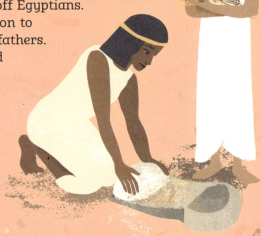

Mother and daughter grinding grain

Only a few children went to school, mostly the sons of well-off Egyptians. Once they had mastered reading and writing, they would go on to train as scribes, doctors, officials and priests, just like their fathers. Some girls from wealthy families also learnt how to read and write, but we don't know whether they went to school like the boys.

Children who didn't go to school helped their parents in the home, in the fields or at the workshop, learning the job they would do when they were older. For girls, this generally meant being taught how to manage the family home: cooking, cleaning, taking care of babies, spinning cloth and mending clothing.

Carpenters making wooden furniture

The school day

Learning to read and write wasn't easy – the Egyptian language was made up of hundreds of different symbols, and children had to learn them all! Week after week, they copied the symbols over and over again, until they were perfect. Papyrus (the Egyptian equivalent of paper) was expensive, so they often practised their writing on pieces of broken pottery called ostraca. As well as reading and writing, children also learnt mathematics and proper behaviour.

Toys

Egyptian toys weren't all that different to toys today. There were dolls, balls, pull-along toys and miniature figures of people or animals made from wood or clay. Some toys had moving parts, such as animal jaws that opened and closed.

Spinning tops

Wooden animal

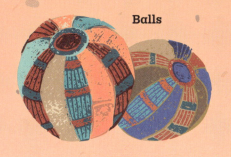

Balls

Play games like an ancient Egyptian!

Children played lots of games, such as wrestling, races and juggling. You could try playing this ancient Egyptian game with your friends. Two people sit on the ground with their legs and arms outstretched, making a barrier. Then, a third person tries to jump over the barrier. The people on the ground can move their arms higher or further apart to make it more of a challenge!

24 HOURS AS AN EGYPTIAN

Life in ancient Egypt was very different for wealthy people and poor people. But this is what might have happened to our well-off Egyptian boy on a typical school day.

6am: wake up

Dedu wakes up at dawn, and has a quick wash before getting dressed. He braids his lock of hair, and applies dark make-up around his eyes.

7am: breakfast

Breakfast is bread and a few dates, washed down with milk. Dedu and his family sit on cushions on the floor and eat using their fingers.

7.30am: offering to the gods

At the family shrine, Dedu's family washes a statue of Bes, the big-bellied god of children, and leaves an offering of food and beer. It's important to keep Bes happy, so he'll watch over the family and keep them safe.

How did Egyptians tell the time?

The ancient Egyptians divided their day into 24 hours: 12 hours of day, and 12 hours of night. People could keep track of the time by looking at the position of the sun and stars in the sky, or by using sundials or simple water clocks – bowls filled with water that leaked out at a certain speed.

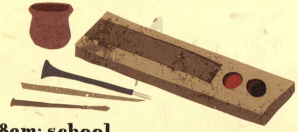

8am: school

Dedu grabs his scribe's equipment – some reed pens, a palette with two holes for red and black ink, and a pot to hold water – and heads off to school, a room attached to the local temple. He joins a row of boys sitting on the floor in front of the teacher and prepares himself for another long, boring day practising writing.

3pm: helping his father

Dedu races home to help his father in his healing room. Sometimes he is allowed to help prepare medicines and ointments for his father's patients.

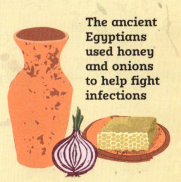

The ancient Egyptians used honey and onions to help fight infections

noon: lunch

After a lunch of bread, cucumber and salted fish, there's time for Dedu to enjoy some wrestling matches with his friends before lessons begin again.

6.30pm: evening

After dinner, Dedu plays a game of Senet with his younger brother, Kyky. He wins, but he's pretty sure he saw Kyky nudge one of his pieces forward when he thought Dedu wasn't looking – he's always cheating.

7pm: evening

Dedu chats to his mother while she gets ready to go to a neighbour's party. She asks the servant girl to fetch her fanciest wig and best jewellery. Dedu wishes he could go too – there'll be acrobats and music and cakes dripping with honey!

8pm: bedtime

It's time for bed. The weather is so hot that Dedu is sleeping on the roof. He lies down on his mat, with his cat, Miu, purring by his side. Soon he's fast asleep.

EVERYDAY JOBS

In ancient Egypt women were the main home-makers, so many of the jobs that took place outside the house were done by men. However, there were also many skilled jobs that women could do – there were female brewers, estate managers, priestesses, doctors, musicians and more. Here are some of the jobs that people did in Egypt.

Farmer

Ploughing, sowing, weeding, watering, harvesting... it was hot, hard work being a farmer! When the river flooded and there was no work to do on the farm, farmers might be sent to do building work for the government instead.

Professional mourner

These women were employed at the funerals of wealthy people. Their job was to join the funeral procession and act as mourners, wailing loudly, throwing dust on their heads and flinging themselves dramatically to the ground.

Getting paid

There were no coins or bank notes in ancient Egyptian times. Instead, workers were paid in goods, using a system of barter. For example, a sandal-maker might exchange a pair of sandals for a sack of grain; a baker could swap a loaf for a few fresh fish; or a carpenter might sell a stool for a goat or a tunic. People who worked for the government were paid in grain, food, clothing and other goods.

Potter

Working as a potter was a mucky job! After softening the clay with their feet, potters shaped it into lots of different objects, from pots and lamps to figurines and even coffins. Like other craftspeople, they sold their goods from their workshops or homes, or at local markets.

Launderer

Most people washed their own clothes, but well-off Egyptians could afford to pay someone else to do it for them. Laundry workers collected clothes door-to-door and washed them in the River Nile.

Scribe

Scribes did lots of different jobs, from writing letters and religious texts to recording practical information, such as tax collection. They worked in all parts of Egypt, from the pharaoh's court to temples, construction sites and local villages.

Artist

The walls of tombs and temples were decorated by teams of artists, who sketched out the design on a grid before filling in the outlines and painting it. Paint was made from ground-up minerals, and paintbrushes were bundles of reeds tied together.

EGYPTIAN WRITING

Egypt was one of the first civilizations in the world to develop a writing system. Instead of letters, it used pictures and symbols called hieroglyphs. There were over 700 of these signs. Imagine how long it would take to learn them all!

Types of writing

For most of its long history, ancient Egypt used two different types of writing:

Hieroglyphs

Hieroglyphs were used for formal writing, such as religious texts or the words carved into temples, tombs and monuments.

Hieratic

A second type of writing, called hieratic, was used for everyday writing, such as official documents. Hieratic symbols were a simplified version of hieroglyphs, so were easier and quicker to write. At school, children started out learning hieratic.

The Rosetta Stone

In 1799, French soldiers in the town of Rosetta in Egypt discovered a large stone slab that had the same message written on it in three languages: hieroglyphs, demotic and ancient Greek. At that time, no one knew how to read hieroglyphs, but the Rosetta Stone helped them crack the code. Scholars could read ancient Greek, so they were able to compare this to the hieroglyphs and figure out what the symbols meant.

Jean-François Champollion used the Rosetta Stone (and other documents) to enable him to decipher hieroglyphs for the first time in 1822.

Later in Egyptian history, a third type of writing sprang up. It was called demotic and it used even simpler symbols.

How to read hieroglyphs

Hieroglyphs could stand for a word or a sound, or both. The hieroglyph that looks like a zigzag, for example (WWWW), was used for the word 'water' but also for the sound 'n'.

To make matters even more complicated, hieroglyph writing could be written in any direction – from left to right, or right to left, but always from top to bottom. The way animal hieroglyphs faced gave the direction of writing. So, for example, you would read the hieroglyphs below from right to left as the animals are facing right.

Hieroglyph alphabet

This picture shows some of the hieroglyphs that most closely match the sounds of our own alphabet. The Egyptians had no hieroglyphs for vowels, so the closest hieroglyphs are shown.

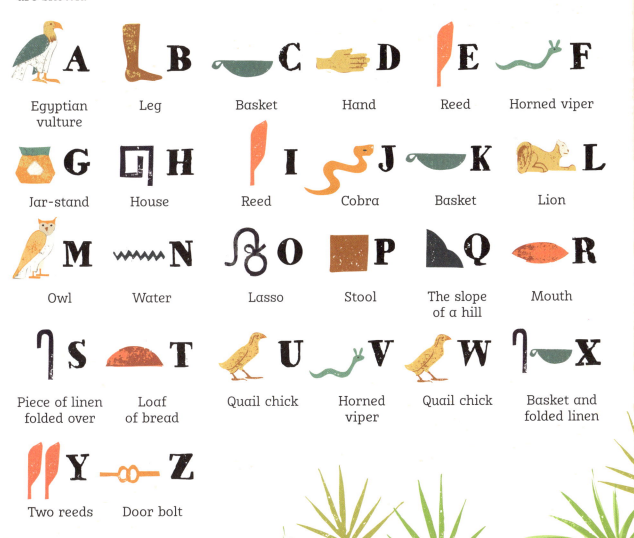

A	B	C	D	E	F
Egyptian vulture	Leg	Basket	Hand	Reed	Horned viper

G	H	I	J	K	L
Jar-stand	House	Reed	Cobra	Basket	Lion

M	N	O	P	Q	R
Owl	Water	Lasso	Stool	The slope of a hill	Mouth

S	T	U	V	W	X
Piece of linen folded over	Loaf of bread	Quail chick	Horned viper	Quail chick	Basket and folded linen

Y	Z
Two reeds	Door bolt

MAKE PAPYRUS PAPER

Papyrus, an early form of paper, was invented by the Egyptians around 3,000 BCE. It was made using the stems of the grass-like papyrus plant, which grew in marshes and along the banks of the Nile River. You can use the same techniques to make your own 'papyrus' paper.

How was papyrus made?

First, workers stripped the outer skin off the stems. Then, they cut the inner part into tissue-thin strips, which were laid out in rows with the edges overlapping. A second set of strips was laid on top, at a right angle, and hammered or pressed together and left to dry. The natural glue in the plant stuck the strips together to form a sheet of papyrus. Sheets could be glued together and rolled up to make long scrolls.

Make your own papyrus

1 Tear up the packaging paper into strips around ¾in (2cm wide) and 12in (30cm) long – you'll need 30–40 of them. In a small container, mix ¼ cup glue with ¼ cup water.

2 Cover your work area in newspaper, and lay the wax paper on top. Dip each strip of brown paper into the glue mixture, running your fingers down the strip to remove any excess glue. Lay the strips side by side on the wax paper, overlapping slightly. Use your fingers to smooth any bumps.

3 Once you have covered the wax paper, begin laying strips in the other direction, at right angles. Leave to dry overnight.

4 Once the brown paper is dry, peel off the wax paper. Your papyrus is ready to decorate! You could draw a picture on it (see box, opposite) or write your name or a secret message using the hieroglyph symbols on page 23.

You will need

- **Brown packaging paper or 2 brown paper bags**
- **Craft glue**
- **Newspaper**
- **Wax paper, around 16 x 16in (40 x 40cm)**
- **Paints or colouring pens**

1

2

3

4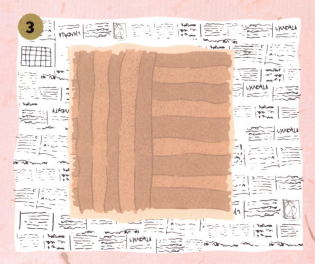

Draw like an ancient Egyptian!

Here's how to draw a figure, the way an Egyptian artist would have done.

1 First, draw a grid measuring 10 rows across and 19 rows down. The shoulders start 3 squares from the top and the waist 8 squares from the top.

2 Draw the head and legs as if you are looking at the person from the side. Draw the chest and arms from the front.

3 Colour in your picture, using the main colours the Egyptians used: red, blue, green, yellow, black and white.

4 If you draw more than one person, make the most important person the biggest in size!

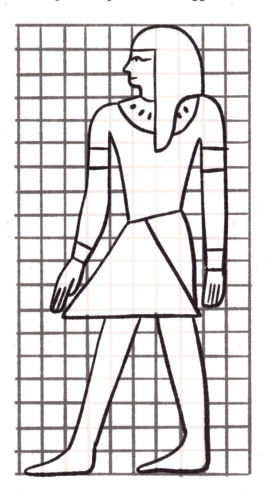

AT SCHOOL

It's nearly the end of the school day, and I'm hot and tired and sticky. With a small sigh, I dip my pen into the ink and draw a neat black line on the shard of broken pottery on my lap. This week we're learning the words for parts of the body. I can almost hear my father's voice telling me to sit up and pay attention. When I'm older, I'll need to know all these words so I can read the medical texts. But it's very hard to concentrate when you've written the same word thirty times already, and it's so hot, and surely it must be time to go home soon, and I wonder if... Ouch!!

I feel the sting of the teacher's switch on my back. "Do you have somewhere else you'd rather be, Dedu?" asks the teacher, sarcastically. "Am I wasting your time teaching you how to write? Perhaps you would rather be a potter, covered in mud? Or a coppersmith, whose fingers are like crocodile claws and who stinks of fish eggs?" I shake my head and stammer an apology. "All of you, repeat after me," he continues. "The scribe is the greatest of all professions!" All around me, I hear twenty voices repeat his words in a loud, sing-song chant. "Nothing is better than writing," the teacher

continues, shaking his finger at me. "The scribe cannot be poor and will never be hungry. Remember that!" Then, with a final glare at me, he waves his hand, dismissing the class.

My friends Irynefer and Paser ask if I want to come to the river, but I've promised to help my father with his patients today. Last week, I learnt how to mix up an eyewash made from honey and onion juice. Today I am hoping he will teach me the magic spell to treat a runny nose and sneezing.

Irynefer's father is an important overseer in charge of one of the big tombs being built on the other side of the river. He says it is so well hidden that no robber will ever be able to find it! Paser's father works at the palace as a scribe. Last month, he was called to the Audience Hall to record all the gifts presented to the pharaoh by a group of Nubians from the south. Paser says there were baskets and baskets of gold, and a strange animal with a towering neck and legs that were taller than me! I think he might be making it up.

Maybe one day, if the gods are willing and I have good fortune, I might become a royal physician and work at the palace too. I really must pay more attention at school. No more day-dreaming...

FASHION

Ancient Egypt had hot summers and mild winters, which meant people didn't need to wear many clothes. In fact, young children and some poor people didn't wear anything at all! Most clothing was made from linen, a light, comfortable material woven from fibres of the flax plant.

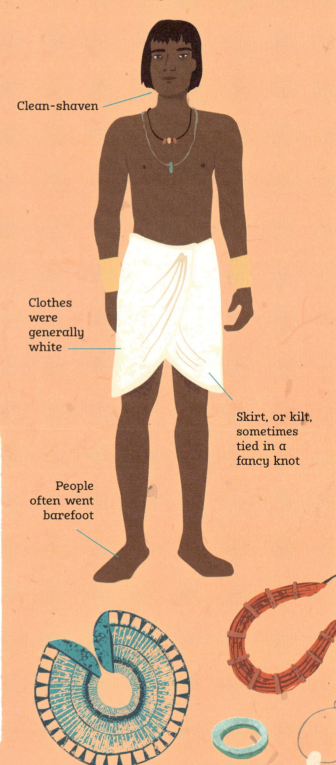

Simple outfit for a man

All men, from pharaohs to farmers, wore wrap-around skirts. The length and style of these changed over the years. In later Egyptian times, wealthier men wore a long tunic over the skirt.

Clean-shaven

Clothes were generally white

Skirt, or kilt, sometimes tied in a fancy knot

People often went barefoot

Looking good

The Egyptians liked to look beautiful, and both women and men wore make-up. Eyes were painted with kohl, made from a dark mineral ground up and mixed with oils. This was thought to keep eyes healthy. Lips were reddened with a paste made from red ochre and animal fat.

Some Egyptians shaved their heads and wore a fancy wig made of human hair instead – the height of fashion! At parties, the wig could be topped with a perfumed wax cone, which slowly melted in the heat and released its scent.

Outfit for a wealthy woman

Women wore long dresses. By the time of the New Kingdom, flowing dresses with sleeves were popular.

Outfit for a pharaoh

One way to tell the pharaoh apart was his headgear. He had several crowns, including a White Crown (representing Upper Egypt) and a Red Crown (representing Lower Egypt).

Wig

Collar made from beads

White crown

Red crown

Long pleated dress made from delicate, see-through linen

Sandals made from papyrus, grass, palm leaves or leather

Ceremonial beard

Nemes – a striped headcloth worn only by the pharaoh

Cloth decorated with gold thread and embroidery

Jewellery

Everyone wore jewellery – men, women and children. The finest pieces were made from precious stones and gold from Egypt's own gold mines. But most people wore simpler jewellery, such as beads made from clay, shells or a glass-like material called faience.

MAKE AN AMULET NECKLACE

The Egyptians didn't just wear jewellery to look good. Sometimes necklaces and bracelets were strung with amulets. These were little objects carved into the shape of gods, animals or other symbols. People believed these objects had magical powers and could protect the wearer from harm or bring them luck. You can make your own amulet necklace.

The Eye of Horus

One of the most popular amulets was the Eye of Horus, which symbolized protection and regeneration. Horus was a falcon god who lost an eye in a battle, which was later restored to him.

You will need

- Old magazine or coloured paper
- Scissors
- Pencil
- Glue stick
- Clear nail polish
- 2oz (50g) air-dry clay
- Toothpick or skewer
- Blunt knife
- Gold, red and blue acrylic paint
- 35in (90cm) length of string

1 Start by making the beads for your necklace. Tear out a few colourful pages from a magazine, and cut them into narrow triangles, around ⅜in (1cm) wide at the base. You'll need around 30 triangles.

2 Lay a triangle on a flat surface, with the coloured side facing down. Place a pencil near the widest end, and apply glue along the length. Then tightly roll the triangle up around itself to form a bead.

3 Slide the bead off the pencil. Repeat the process to make the rest of the beads.

4 Apply a thin layer of clear nail polish to each bead. Leave them to stand on one end until they are dry.

5 To make your Eye of Horus amulet, roll out your clay until it is ³⁄₁₆in (5mm) thick. Then use a toothpick or skewer to draw the amulet design, following the step-by-step drawings opposite. Don't cut too deeply into the clay – your marks should be very light.

6 Cut out the amulet using a blunt knife, then make a hole at the top by pushing a pencil all the way through. Leave to dry.

7 Once the clay is dry, you can paint your amulet.

8 When the paint is dry, thread the amulet and the beads onto the string, and tie the two ends together. Your necklace is ready to wear – may the Eye of Horus protect you!

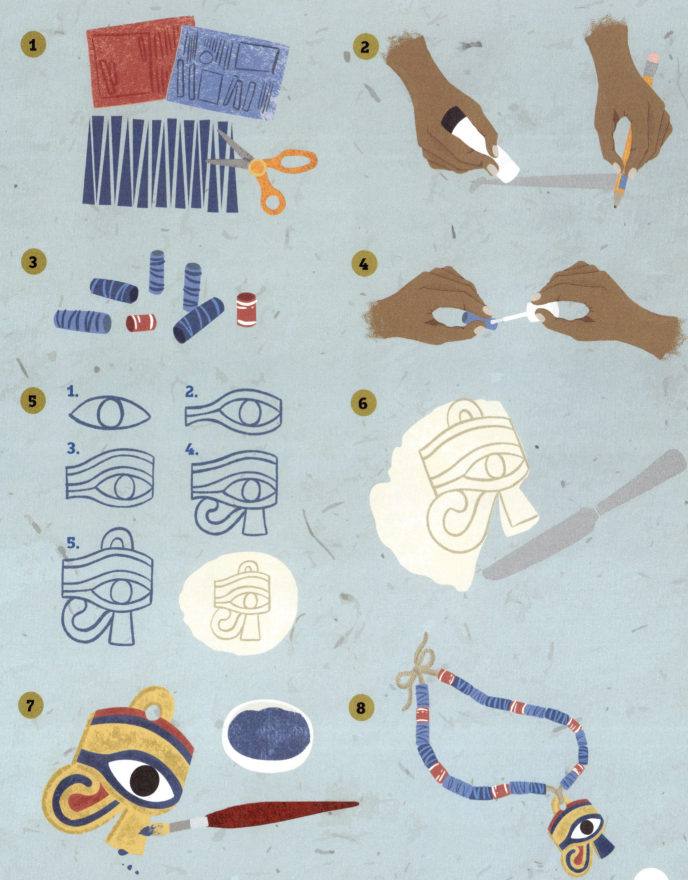

GODS AND TEMPLES

The Egyptians worshipped hundreds of gods and goddesses. They thought these gods kept the world in balance, and had special powers over different parts of people's lives, from music and writing to childbirth and death. This meant everyone worked hard to keep the gods happy!

Homes of the gods

Egyptian temples were important and secret places. Only priests, priestesses and pharaohs were allowed inside. Each temple was home to a god or gods, who were believed to live inside statues housed in the innermost sanctuary of the temple. Every morning, the high priest 'woke up' the statue so it could be washed, dressed in clean clothes and left offerings of food.

Ordinary people made their own offerings to the gods in smaller shrines in their homes or other places. Everybody got a chance to see the gods at religious festivals, when the statues were paraded through the streets. Along the way, people could ask the gods questions: the priests carrying the platform holding the statue gave the god's answer by tipping the platform forward for 'yes', or backward for 'no'.

Priests and priestesses

Some temples were huge complexes where hundreds of priests and priestesses lived and worked, serving the gods. As well as the powerful high priest, there were lower priests who did different jobs, such as looking after the temple, carrying out funeral rituals, keeping records or writing religious texts.

Gods and goddesses

Here are some of the most important gods and goddesses.

Some gods and goddesses were shown with the heads or bodies of animals that lived in Egypt.

Ra - The sun god

Thoth - God of writing and wisdom. The Egyptians believed he invented hieroglyphs

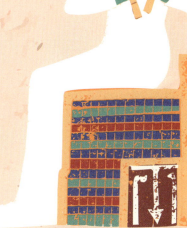

Osiris - God of the underworld, who greeted the dead in the afterlife

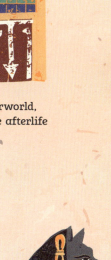

Isis - Important goddess of motherhood and magic

Anubis - Jackal-headed god of the dead and mummification

Horus - The falcon-headed god of the sky, war, hunting and kingship. Son of Isis and Osiris

Bastet - Goddess of cats, fertility and childbirth. The Egyptians thought cats were sacred animals

Sekhmet - Lioness goddess of war and healing

DEATH AND THE AFTERLIFE

The ancient Egyptians didn't think that life ended with death. They believed in an afterlife, where a person could live again in paradise – so long as they had lived a good life, kept the gods happy and made all the right preparations.

The Field of Reeds

The Egyptian afterlife, called the Field of Reeds, was a perfect version of Egypt, with fields of golden crops and boats sailing along sky-blue rivers. Here, people could spend time with their friends and families, eat their favourite foods and live happily ever after. Pictures of the afterlife were painted onto the walls of tombs to help guide the dead there.

Journey to the afterlife

An afterlife wasn't guaranteed, so it was important to prepare. Here's some advice on how to make it to paradise in ancient Egypt!

1. First, your spirit will need a body in the afterlife. You can pay a priest to mummify your body to preserve it for as long as possible (see pages 40–41). The priests will know all the right spells to say while your body is being prepared and buried, to help it travel to the next life.

Shabti figures

2. You might want to be buried with some useful things for the next life, such as clothes and make-up. And you'll definitely need some shabti figures. These little models of servants will do all the hard work for you in the afterlife, like cooking and making beer, so you can put your feet up and relax.

**Part of a
Book of the Dead papyrus**

3. Your spirit will face a dangerous journey through the underworld to reach the Field of Reeds. Make sure you have the right spells with you in your tomb – they could be written on your coffin, or on a papyrus scroll called the *Book of the Dead*. These secret spells will help you overcome any obstacles and challenges.

Medicine

Life was short in ancient Egypt – disease, accidents, childbirth and war meant that most people only lived until their 30s. Egyptian doctors used a mix of medicines, magic spells and prayers to treat injuries and illnesses. Some remedies probably did more harm than good – for example, wounds were bandaged up with raw meat, and eye problems were sometimes treated with mixtures made from animal dung or blood!

4. Once you're safely buried, make sure your family or a priest performs daily offerings at your tomb, so that you can carry on living peacefully in paradise.

JOURNEY TO THE UNDERWORLD

I'm up on the roof with my mother and little sister, when I hear the sound of wailing and sobbing, getting louder and louder. Peering down to the street below, I see a procession moving slowly towards the river. It must be the funeral of Neferhotep, one of our neighbours, who died two months ago. I've heard the builders have just finished his tomb on the other side of the river. I can see his wife, and some of the priests from the temple. The coffin lies on a sledge, pulled by several men, their bodies glistening with sweat. Other men are carrying baskets piled high with Neferhotep's belongings, and food for the funeral feast. Women hired for the funeral shriek and sob and fling themselves to the ground, throwing handfuls of dust over their heads.

"It's Neferhotep, on his way to Duat," I call to my mother over my shoulder. My little sister, Merit, looks up. "Where is Duat?" she asks.

My mother pulls Merit onto her knee. "Before Neferhotep can reach the afterlife," she begins, "his spirit must travel to Duat, the underworld. It is a place of many dangers. Once the ferryman of the gods has carried Neferhotep across the great river, he will reach a land of parched deserts and lakes of fire, where terrible monsters roam. He must pass through twelve gates, each guarded by a fierce gatekeeper and giant snakes that spit poison and flames. To make it through safely, he must speak the name of each guardian."

"But Neferhotep will have all the right spells to help him," I break in, seeing my sister looking worried. "Yes," smiles my mother, "The *Book of the Dead* will help guide him past the dangers to the Hall of the Two Truths, where the great god Osiris sits on the throne. There, 42 judges will ask Neferhotep if he has done any wrongdoing in his life, like telling lies or stealing."

"What happens if he once told a very small lie?" my little sister asks, her lip trembling. I look at her suspiciously, and suddenly remember my spinning top that got broken last week – I knew it was her! My mother kisses her cheek. "Telling lies is very wrong," she says, "but the *Book of the Dead* will tell him the right spells to say and keep him safe. Then there is one more test to come. Neferhotep's heart will be placed on the scales and weighed against the Feather of Truth. If he has led a good life, the scales will balance and he will pass into the Field of Reeds and live in paradise. But if his heart is heavier than the feather, it will be gobbled up by Ammut, a goddess with the head of a crocodile, the legs of a hippo and the body of a lion."

"And everyone knows," I add, "that Ammut's favourite food is little girls' hearts, especially annoying ones who break their brother's toys!"

TOMBS AND PYRAMIDS

Where you were buried in ancient Egypt depended on how well-off you were. Some people ended up in simple pits in the desert, others in fancy tombs carved into rocky hillsides. If you were a pharaoh with thousands of men at your command, you could afford a really spectacular tomb: a towering pyramid!

Pyramid power

Pyramids were built to protect the body and treasures of a pharaoh after he had died, so that he could be reunited with them in the afterlife. These huge, magnificent monuments, visible for miles around, also made sure the pharaoh would never be forgotten. Building a pyramid took years – so long, in fact, that some pharaohs died before their pyramid was finished.

The Great Pyramid contains over 2 million giant blocks of stone. Stone masons cut the stone blocks from the ground and used a chisel and hammer to shape them so that they fitted together perfectly.

The Great Pyramid

The three most famous Egyptian pyramids were built at Giza. The largest is Pharaoh Khufu's Great Pyramid, which was finished around 2550 BCE.

Secret rock tombs

By the time of the New Kingdom, pyramids had gone out of fashion. Instead, pharaohs built themselves smaller, secret tombs carved into the rock in a remote, guarded valley now known as the Valley of the Kings. They hoped their buried treasures would be safe from grave robbers there. But over the years most of these tombs, like the pyramids, were stripped of their riches.

It's thought the Great Pyramid took over 20 years to build and involved 20,000 workers – quarry workers, stone masons, ramp builders, tool-makers and more. They might well have thought it an honour to help build the tomb of their pharaoh, who was seen as a living god.

The rough inner stones of the pyramid were covered by smooth, angled stones made from white limestone. Only a few of these have survived, at the foot of the pyramid. When it was first built, the entire Great Pyramid would have gleamed a dazzling, brilliant white!

The massive stone blocks were moved on large wooden sledges. No one knows for sure exactly how they were raised up the pyramid, but most archaeologists think they were probably hauled up on ramps, perhaps using levers and a simple pulley system.

EGYPTIAN MUMMIES

Mummifying bodies was a way of preserving them for the afterlife. Not everyone could afford to be mummified, and there were also different levels of mummification to choose from. The process described below was the deluxe version for the wealthy.

Making a mummy

Mummifying a body could take around 70 days. The priest in charge of the rituals wore a jackal mask to turn himself into Anubis, the god of death and mummification.

1 First, the body was washed and all the organs except the heart were removed. The brain was pulled out in mushy pieces through the nose, using a special hook. The liver, lungs, intestines and stomach were placed in four special containers called canopic jars.

2 The hollow body was filled and covered with a salt called natron, which helped to dry it out. This might take 40 days.

3 After the salt was removed, the body was cleaned with scented oils and packed with linen or sawdust.

4 Make-up was applied. Any missing body parts might be replaced with artificial versions made from wood or metal.

5 The body was wrapped in a lot of linen – sometimes hundreds of square metres! Protective amulets were placed into the wrappings.

6 Finally, a mask was put over the head and the body was placed in a coffin. Some wealthy people had more than one coffin, one inside the other.

Canopic jars

Hook to remove the brain

MAKE A MUMMIFIED ORANGE

Mummification worked by drying out the body. You can have a go at mummifying an orange in the same way.

You will need

- An orange
- Teaspoon
- Kitchen towel
- 3½oz (100g) salt
- 3½oz (100g) bicarbonate of soda
- 1 tsp cinnamon
- A few cloves
- Permanent marker
- 30in (80cm) length of bandage

1

2

3

1 Make a slit in the orange, then use a teaspoon to scoop out all the flesh. Stuff the inside of the orange with kitchen towel for a few minutes to absorb any moisture.

2 Mix the salt, bicarbonate of soda, cinnamon and cloves together, then spoon this mixture into the orange. If you like, you can draw a face on your orange now!

3 Pushing the slit together, wrap the orange tightly with the bandage, tucking in the end. Leave it in a warm, dry place for a couple of months. When you unwrap your orange, it will be dark, dry and withered – just like an Egyptian mummy!

FUN AND GAMES

Just like us, people in ancient Egypt liked to have fun playing board games, listening to music, competing in sports and going to parties. Not everyone had the same amount of free time though. Most ordinary people worked almost every day, but everyone got days off for religious holidays.

Board games

People of all ages and classes enjoyed playing board games – even the poorest Egyptian could scratch a grid into the sand and find some pebbles to use for pieces. One of the most popular games was Senet, which involved two players racing their pieces across a board of squares. Instead of dice, players used knuckle bones (knobbly animal bones) or 'throwing sticks' that were painted light on one side and dark on the other.

Music and parties

In the evenings, wealthier Egyptians sometimes hosted banquets. Guests were entertained by musicians playing harps, flutes, cymbals and other instruments, while dancing girls showed off their acrobatic moves.

Lute

Harp

Double pipes

Festivals

Religious festivals were a time for everyone, rich and poor, to let their hair down. On these special occasions, images of the gods were sometimes taken from temples and carried through the streets, joined by musicians, singers, dancers and acrobats. People gathered to watch the procession and feast on the free bread and beer provided by the temple. Some festivals lasted for days.

Outdoor sports and games

The Egyptians spent a lot of time outdoors. They went sailing on the River Nile, swam, fished, hunted and played lots of different sports, including a game of tug-of-war and wrestling. Which of these ancient Egyptian sports would you enjoy doing most?

Ball catching game

Gymnastics

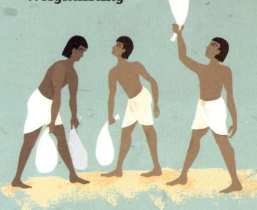

Tug-of-war

Weightlifting

Wrestling

Rowing

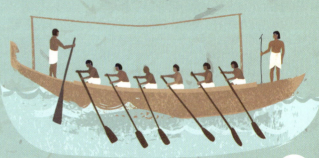

MAKE A BOARD GAME

Mehen, or the Game of the Snake, was played 5,000 years ago, making it one of the world's oldest known games. Over time, the rules have been lost, but it's thought to have been a race game, a bit like snakes and ladders. Make your own Mehen board and pieces, and challenge a friend!

You will need

- Thick card
- A pencil
- Paint
- Colouring pens
- 4 lolly sticks
- Coin

1 First make your board – a coiled snake. Draw around a large plate onto thick card and cut out the circle. Use a pencil to draw a spiral onto the circle, ending with a snake's head, then divide it up into around 20 segments. Paint your board or colour it in.

2 Now make the playing pieces. Draw around a coin onto thick card to make eight circles, and cut them out. Colour them in on both sides: four one colour, and four another colour. On each set, draw a lion's face on one counter, and little people on the other three counters, leaving the reverse sides plain.

3 This game uses throw sticks instead of dice. To make them, take four lolly sticks and paint one side a dark colour.

How to use throw sticks

Throw the sticks into the air. When they land, count the number of dark sides. This is the number of places you can move.

Mehen can be played by more people – just make extra sets of counters.

How to play

There have been lots of guesses about how Mehen was played. This version of the game is based on some of these ideas.

Each player has three people counters and one lion. The aim is to race your people from the snake's tail to its head and back to the start. But watch out – lions might be prowling!

- Throw the sticks to see who goes first, then take turns.

- Players need to throw a 1 to move a person counter onto the tail (the starting square).

- Each turn, you can choose to move a counter or (if you throw a 1) place a new counter on the board.

- You can only reach the snake's head with an exact throw. Once a counter arrives there, turn it over. It can now begin its journey back to the start.

- As soon as your first person counter reaches the snake's head, you can release your lion! Move it straight onto the snake's tail.

- Each turn, you can choose whether to move your lion or one of your people. If your lion lands on an opponent's counter, it eats the person and that counter has to go all the way back to the tail and begin again.

- The winner is the first player to get all three people to the snake's head and back again. You don't need an exact throw to get off the board.

A DAY ON THE RIVER

Today, my father has taken me and my older sister, Nefret, boating on the river. He has brought throwing sticks with him to hunt birds. I think my father is hoping to impress my mother by bringing home a duck, but I've seen him hunt before and his aim is terrible.

I love it out here in the marshes. The water laps gently against our boat as we drift through the reeds. Every so often, a dragonfly darts overhead. On the far bank I see a flock of ibis wading in the shallows, dipping their long beaks into the water.

Suddenly, three wild ducks flutter up from the reeds with a great whirr of wings. I clamber forward on the boat, holding my father's legs steady as he takes aim with his stick. But just as he is drawing back his arm there is a loud shout. Distracted, he drops his stick with a clatter and the birds fly away, squawking.

I look around to see two fishing boats drawing close to each other. One man is calling out to the other boat and brandishing his long punting pole. My father tells us the man is suggesting a friendly jousting competition. Sure enough, soon the rival fishermen are trading good-natured insults and trying to push each other into the water with their poles. It doesn't take long before one man loses his footing and tumbles into the water. The others erupt into cheers as he comes splashing to the surface, cursing loudly. It looks fun. I suggest to my sister we could try some river jousting too, but she just gives me a withering look that makes my father laugh.

Soon the fishing boats drift away up the river and everything is peaceful again. A frog croaks nearby, and in the distance I can hear marshmen singing as they gather great bundles of papyrus further along the river. I lie back and close my eyes...

The next thing I know I'm in the river, spluttering and coughing. Wiping my eyes, I see a huge mouth looming over me, its enormous teeth as long as my arm. It must have surfaced from the water and made a wave big enough to knock me into the river. The great beast turns and lumbers away through the reeds: a hippo! Looking around me, I see my father and sister still on the boat, calling out to me. Nefret is pointing to the far bank, where I catch a glimpse of a crocodile's tail slipping into the water. Quick, back to the boat!

Soon, my father is hauling me on board and wrapping his arms around me. My teeth are chattering with fear. What a close escape! The gods must have been looking after me. "Time to go home, I think," my father smiles. "No ducks for your mother today. Next time I'll catch twenty, I'm sure."

FOOD AND DRINK

The rich soil left behind by the River Nile's yearly floods meant farmers could grow plenty of grain to make into bread and beer – Egypt's two most important foods. Most of the time, there was plenty to go round and nobody had to go hungry. But some people ate better than others.

Food for the poor

Poorer Egyptians ate quite simple food: mainly bread and vegetables. From time to time, there might be some meat as a special treat. Water wasn't always clean and safe, so everyone drank beer instead, even children! It was thick, soup-like and filling.

Food was very important in Egyptian society. It was offered to the gods, buried with the dead in their tombs, and used as a form of payment for many workers.

Food for the rich

Wealthy people enjoyed a much more varied diet, including plenty of roasted and grilled meat, cakes and pastries sweetened with honey and fruit, and imported luxuries such as wines and olive or sesame oils. They drank beer, like everyone else, but could also afford wine.

Eating etiquette

We don't know exactly how ancient Egyptians ate their food, but they probably mostly used their fingers and may even have used flatbread to scoop things up, as modern Egyptians sometimes do.

How do we know?

The Egyptians didn't leave behind any recipe books, but scenes painted on the walls of tombs show the foods people ate, and even some of the ways they prepared and cooked it. Archaeologists have also found food remains in tombs and other sites – including a 3,200-year -old cheese that's thought to be the oldest ever found! There are still many things we don't know though, such as how many meals a day people ate.

A wall painting from the tomb of the vizier Rekhmira showing workmen producing bread dough.

Milk from cows and goats was drunk fresh or turned into cheese or yogurt.

Thick, cloudy beer was made from barley and wheat. It was sometimes drunk though a straw, which had a filter at the end to sieve out the sediment.

Beer

Fish could be dried or salted to make it last longer in the hot climate.

Honeycomb

Tiger nuts

Cheese

Figs

Fish

Dates

Goose

Watermelon

Radishes

Garlic

Lettuce

Beans

Lentils

Onions

Bread

Many people used honey to sweeten food.

Bread was made from emmer wheat or barley. There were lots of different types, from simple flatbreads to fancy fruit loaves.

Ducks, geese, sheep, goats and pigs were raised for their meat. Beef was expensive so was only eaten by the wealthy – or offered to the gods.

EGYPTIAN RECIPES

The Egyptian diet was pretty simple, and many people ate the same foods from one day to the next. Do you think you would have enjoyed eating and drinking like an Egyptian? Try out these recipes and see.

Bread

Egyptian bread came in lots of different flavours and shapes. Bakers sometimes even shaped their dough into the figures of animals! This bread is in the shape of a fierce Nile crocodile.

Makes 2 crocodiles

Ingredients

- 10½oz (300g) wholemeal flour
- 1 tsp dry yeast
- 1 tsp salt
- 8½fl oz (250ml) warm water
- 2 tbsp honey
- 4 small raisins or seeds

1 Mix the dry ingredients together in a large bowl. Dissolve the honey in the warm water and mix it into the dry ingredients. Knead the dough on a floured work surface for 10 minutes.

2 Place the dough in the bowl, cover with a tea towel and leave in a warm place for 1 hour.

3 Preheat the oven to 220°C (fan 200°C). Set aside a small piece of dough (this will be used in the next step), then divide the rest into two. Shape each piece into a crocodile.

4 Use small pieces of dough to form feet and add small raisins or seeds for the eyes.

5 Use a pair of scissors to snip into the back of the crocodiles to form scales. Snip into the feet to make claws. Using a toothpick or skewer, poke two holes to make nostrils.

6 Bake on a tray in the oven for 20 minutes.

Tiger nut cones

A 3,500-year-old painting in an Egyptian tomb shows this sweet treat being made. This has allowed Egyptologists to make a guess at the recipe. Here is one possibility.

Makes 10 cones

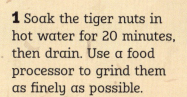

Ingredients

- **5oz (150g) peeled tiger nuts**
- **1¾oz (50g) butter**
- **3½oz (100g) honey**
- **3½oz (100g) finely chopped dates**

1 Soak the tiger nuts in hot water for 20 minutes, then drain. Use a food processor to grind them as finely as possible.

2 Heat the butter, honey, dates and ground tiger nuts in a saucepan on a low heat for five minutes, stirring regularly.

3 Leave the mixture until cool enough to handle (about 20–30 minutes). Roll small amounts of the mixture in your hands to make little balls, then shape into cones.

Tiger nuts are root vegetables that grow in Africa. You can buy them online or from some health food shops.

Cottage cheese

One of the cheeses the ancient Egyptians ate may have been similar to cottage cheese, a soft cheese that is still eaten in Egypt today.

Ingredients

- **17fl oz (500ml) milk**
- **2 tbsp lemon juice**
- **½ tsp salt**

1 Heat the milk in a saucepan until the edges start to foam.

2 Remove from the heat and add the lemon juice. Stir a couple of times, then leave to rest for 30 minutes. The milk will separate into solid parts (curds) and liquid (whey).

3 Pour the mixture over a sieve lined with cheesecloth or a clean tea towel. Leave to drain for 15 minutes.

4 Gather up the cloth around the curds to form a ball. Rinse it under cold water, then squeeze all the liquid out.

5 Tip the curds into a bowl, break them up and mix in the salt.

COULD YOU HAVE LIVED LIKE AN ANCIENT EGYPTIAN?

In some ways, the ancient Egyptian way of life wasn't so different to ours. Men and women went to work, spent time with their families, and played sports and board games in their free time. But in other ways, the Egyptians lived very differently to us. Think about the questions here and talk about your answers with a friend, parent, carer or teacher.

1 Only a very small number of children went to school in ancient Egypt. Most children helped their parents instead, learning the skills needed to do their job. Do you think you would enjoy a childhood like this? What would you like and dislike about it? Would you prefer to go to school and learn how to read and write?

2 Instead of coins and paper money, the Egyptians used a system of bartering. Goods were valued according to a unit called a 'deben', which was a certain weight of copper. For example, a tunic worth 5 deben could be exchanged for 5-deben worth of wheat. Imagine you want to buy the five items listed opposite.

For each one, can you think of an item in your home with a similar value that you could offer in exchange?

- Loaf of bread
- Book
- Pair of shoes
- Bicycle
- Umbrella

3 If you time-travelled back to ancient Egyptian times, what three things do you think you would miss the most from your modern-day life? It might be a particular gadget or toy, an activity you like to do, or a comfort like a soft pillow! Is there anything you'd like to take from the time of the Egyptians and bring back to the modern world?

4 In ancient Egypt, women were equal with men in law and had many rights (see page 10). But men still ran the government, and women were expected to look after the family home. Do you think women got a fair deal? How do their lives compare to the lives of women today?

5 Many ordinary Egyptians ate exactly the same foods every day – bread, beer and vegetables. How would you feel eating these same few foods, day after day after day? Which foods from the modern day would you miss the most?

6 The Egyptians had lots of different gods for all the things that were important in their lives, from the sun and rain to writing and motherhood. Make up a new Egyptian god or goddess for something that is important to you. Give your god a name, and choose an animal to represent them; for example, a goddess of friendship might have the head of a dog, because dogs are loyal.

7 Some jobs in ancient Egypt were hard work, dirty or downright dangerous. Which of the following would you rather be?

- **Labourer** – the work is exhausting and injuries are common, but the government gives you food and a roof over your head.
- **Soldier** – you might get the chance to rise up the ranks, if you can survive the long hours of training, strict army discipline and fighting in battles.
- **Embalmer** – preserving dead bodies is an important but messy job. You need a strong stomach to remove brains through a nose with a hook!
- **Farmer's wife** – you are busy from morning to night grinding grain, cooking, making clothes, looking after children and helping in the fields.
- **Fisherman** – working with fish all day is stinky, and the risk of being attacked by a crocodile or hippo is just part of the job!

GLOSSARY

afterlife
A place where some people believe you go after death.

archaeologist
A person who studies how humans lived in the past by looking at the things they left behind, such as pottery, tools and buildings.

amulet
A small charm thought to protect the wearer from harm.

ancestors
The people from whom you are descended, such as your great-grandparents, great-great-grandparents, and other people further back in time.

Assyrian empire
A huge and powerful kingdom in ancient Mesopotamia, a region that is now part of Iraq. It existed from perhaps as long ago as 2500 BCE to around 600 BCE.

bartering
Exchanging goods or services without using money.

civil war
A war fought between people of the same country or land.

civilization
A large group of people who share a similar culture and way of life, such as shared laws and a shared language.

Egyptologist
A person who studies ancient Egypt.

empire
A large area of different lands and peoples, all ruled by one person or government.

estate manager
A person who manages a large farm.

fertile
If soil is fertile, it means plants can grow easily in it.

figurine
A small statue of a person, god or animal.

grindstone
A stone used for milling (grinding) grain into flour. The upper stone was moved forwards and backwards against a lower stone, crushing the grain.

hieroglyphs
Picture symbols used to write words and sounds.

high priest
The most important and powerful priest in a temple.

Hittites
An ancient people who ruled over an empire in what is now Turkey and Syria. Their civilization was at its greatest between 1600 BCE and 1200 BCE.

irrigate
Adding water to fields to help crops grow.

mummy
A body that has been preserved after death.

New Kingdom
The period between c.1550 BCE and c.1075 BCE, when Egypt was at its largest size.

obelisk
A tall, four-sided stone column with a pointed tip, decorated with carvings and hieroglyphs. Obelisks were placed in temples, often in pairs in front of gateways, to honour the sun-god.

papyrus
A reed-like riverside plant. The Egyptians used papyrus to make rope, boats, sandals and a paper-like material for writing on.

Persian empire
An ancient empire based in what is now Iran. For around 200 years, from 550 BCE, it ruled a huge area including parts of southern Asia, northern Africa and southern Europe.

pharaoh
The title given to the all-powerful rulers of ancient Egypt. The word pharaoh means 'great house'.

pyramid
Huge stone structure with a square base and four sloping sides that meet at a point. Egypt's pyramids were built as tombs or memorials for the pharaohs.

quarries
Large pits where rocks, sand or other materials are dug out of the ground, to be used for building.

ritual
A ceremony in which a sequence of actions are done in the same way every time.

scribe
A person in ancient Egypt who knew how to read and write. Scribes kept ancient Egypt running, and were highly respected.

serfs
In medieval Europe, serfs were farmers who worked the land of the local lord. They had to obey the landowner and were not free to move away. In exchange for their work, they were allowed to farm small pieces of land for themselves.

shrine
A sacred place that housed a statue of a god, where offerings could be left.

slave
A woman, man or child who is owned as property by someone else, and made to work.

sundial
An instrument that tells the time of day by the position of a shadow cast on the surface of the sundial, which has markings for each hour of daylight.

tax
A payment given to the government to pay for services it provides. In ancient Egypt, officials collected tax in the form of grain, cattle and other goods. The grain was used to pay government workers, traded with neighbouring lands or stored to feed the people in years of drought.

underworld
The place where Egyptians believed they went after they died. It was also known as Duat.

Valley of the Kings
A remote valley near the ancient city of Thebes (modern-day Luxor) where, from around 1500 BCE, pharaohs were buried in secret tombs.

vizier
The pharaoh's second-in-command.

ABOUT THE AUTHOR

Claire Saunders has been writing and editing books for more than 20 years. Specializing in children's non-fiction, she has authored or co-authored many titles including *The Power Book*, *The Birthday Almanac*, *A World of Gratitude* and various activity books, including *The Great British Staycation Activity Book*, the *Football Fantastic Activity Book* and the *Only in America Activity Book*. Claire has also written *Live Like a Roman* and *Live Like a Viking* for Button books. A graduate of Cambridge University, she has previously worked for Ivy Press and Rough Guides and still loves travelling the world, learning about the history of other cultures. She lives with her family in Lewes, southern England.

Acknowledgements

With thanks to Professor Ian Shaw, Senior Research Fellow (University of Liverpool), for his expert knowledge and help.

First published 2024 by Button Books, an imprint of Guild of Master Craftsman Publications Ltd, Castle Place, 166 High Street, Lewes, East Sussex, BN7 1XU, UK. Text © Claire Saunders, 2024. Copyright in the Work © GMC Publications Ltd, 2024. ISBN 978 1 78708 154 3. Distributed by Publishers Group West in the United States. All rights reserved. The right of Claire Saunders to be identified as the author of this work has been asserted in accordance with the Copyright, Designs and Patents Act 1988, sections 77 and 78. No part of this publication may be reproduced, stored in a retrieval system, or transmitted in any form or by any means without the prior permission of the publisher and copyright owner. The publishers and author can accept no legal responsibility for any consequences arising from the application of information, advice, or instructions given in this publication. A catalogue record for this book is available from the British Library. Publisher: Jonathan Bailey, Production: Jim Bulley, Senior Project Editor: Susie Behar, Designer: Emily Hurlock, Illustrator: Ruth Hickson. Additional illustration: Emily Hurlock. Colour origination by GMC Reprographics. Printed and bound in China.

FSC
www.fsc.org
MIX
Paper | Supporting responsible forestry
FSC® C144853

Button Books

For more on Button Books, contact:
GMC Publications Ltd, Castle Place,
166 High Street, Lewes, East Sussex,
BN7 1XU, United Kingdom
Tel: +44 (0)1273 488005
buttonbooks.co.uk/buttonbooks.us